I0844767

''E' come vedere un film ad occhi chiusi''

"It's like watching a movie with your eyes closed"

Giulia Segreti

''Con la voce si può fare tutto''

"You can do everything with your voice"

Barone Mark Kheel

AN EROTIC AUDIOREADER

GIULIA SEGRETI

QR CODE YOUTUBE "GIULIA SEGRETI"

Biography

Giulia Segreti was born on January 6, 1992 in Fermo and lives in Torre San Patrizio with her partner. He studied acting for 4 years and attended a dubbing course in Rome. In 2012 she opened her YouTube channel.

Marco Cognigni was born in Ancona on 11 July 1993. He graduated from the faculty of mathematics and applications in Camerino and currently teaches in several high schools. Since 2014 he has collaborated with Giulia Segreti in the creation of audio-readings and dubbing on YouTube.

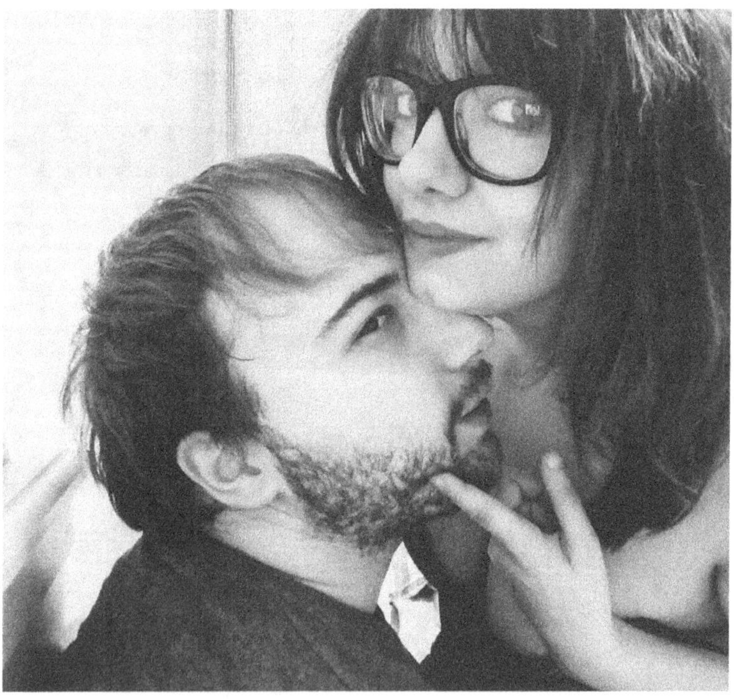

Where to Find Us

Our Social Networks

-YOUTUBE   @giuliasegreti

-FACEBOOK   @giuliasegreti   @baronemarkkheel

-FACEBOOK PAGE   @giuliasegreti   @BMK's Room

-INSTAGRAM   @giuliasegreti   @baronemarkkheel

-TIKTOK   @giuliasegreti

Hello!

You must be wondering: Who are you? What are you doing on youtube? What are Audio Readings? How do you make them? How important is the voice? I read that right ... Erotic Audioleggios? How did you get here? Whose is the male voice? Are you engaged? Are you voice actors? How long have you been on youtube?

There are many questions :)

In this short book / guide I will tell you about my path and the audio-readings of novels by Italian writers and beyond! Also about how to exploit your potential on social media, mainly YouTube.

You will find free contests only for those who have the book so that you can also make your emerging novel known in my channel!

I want to take you on this journey! Get to know me :)

How we met

This is one of the most requested questions on the web!

How did this all start?

How did you meet?

First of all, I had recently begun to approach this type of special audio-reading.

Starting precisely with the Shadowhunters saga.

I was looking for a voice that would get me excited for the role of the character of JACE WAYLAND!

So I went in search of my " Jace " in a group that dealt with dubbing and vocals.

To be honest, in that group I found only horrible, unprepared and immature voices.

Then in the end " I saw " ... him!

it looks like the beginning of the After novel so called but it really happened;)

BARON MARK KHEEL

Yes, first of all, the name struck me ... a bit strange and mysterious.

Then later after listening to his voice I was immediately convinced!

I liked it and it reflected my vision of the character in the novels well.

So I chose him!

Of course he had to improve something but thanks to me he succeeded.

Thus began the various collaborations that you can also see on my youtube channel!

Let's talk about readings since 2014!

Little by little we both improved in terms of interpretation.

I was immediately very happy to have found a friend who then had the same passions as me.

It was now the male part of all my reading.

One day I also discovered that we were almost neighbors.

30 minutes away from where I was.

Then as the months went by, we went out more and more often.

We shared a passion for dubbing, reading and youtube.

We also did a lot of live shows together on FB and Youtube!

Together we also gave life to our first show at the theater which dealt with short interpretations of readings from novels:

- TFIOS [the fault of the stars]

- Shadowhunters

- Write me again.

The show lasted about 2 HOURS :)

It was great!

And I thank Mom Marisa for allowing all of this!

Then that evening, when we were dismantling the show together with the sound engineer, he ventures by asking Barone an uncomfortable question:

" I see you well together. Do you like her?"

Baron confesses:

"Of course yes. You know I like it. I always tell him. "

Honestly, I only saw a beautiful friendship.

I was afraid of finding out where all this would lead me and I didn't care about a relationship.

And here I ... I cannot fail to mention a friend and fan of ours Giorgia Russo.

For those who have followed us from the beginning, you have certainly seen our crazy lives always on my youtube channel and sometimes a week we met to talk about novels, audio-readings and general " scleri ".

The live youtubes are called " Giulia's Lounge " and I hope to continue them in the future.

In these LIVE, Barone continued and continued to try with me.

However, in the end, one evening, after having edited one of our " dubbing " on a reading, I called him.

Our call ended at 3 in the NIGHT!

We talked a lot.

I gambled a game.

It was a series of questions each to get to know each other better but only telling the truth.

Eventually we got to talk about the " KISS ".

I never gave in my life ... maybe in elementary school !! hahaha

Neither did he. But let's talk about a real kiss!

The next evening, there was a gentle, slow kiss.

From then on ... we're officially engaged.

As the days passed, something was being born in me ...

I had listened to my heart.

In short, in the end, our relationship is consolidated more and more.

Of course even with ups and downs like all couples.

He opened my world ...

... and I yours.

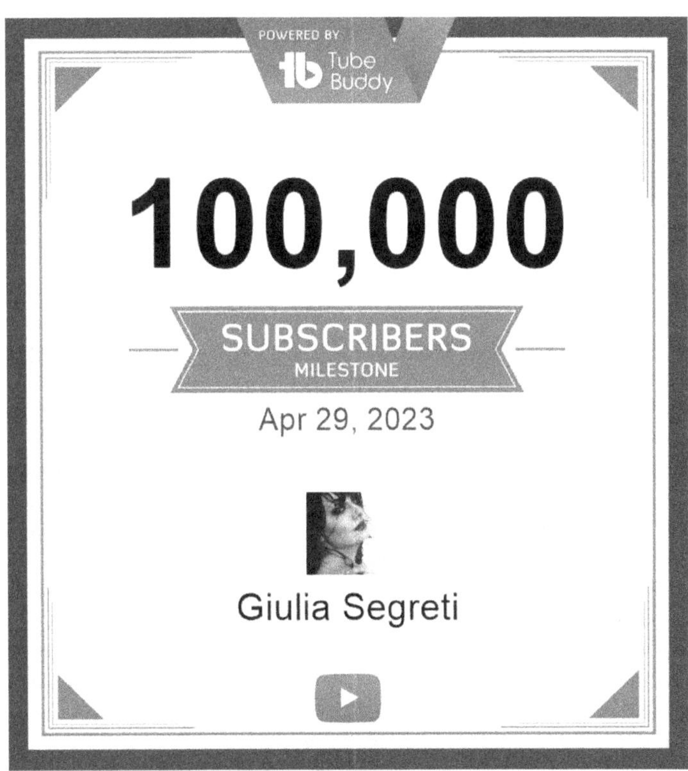

POWERED BY
tb Tube Buddy
100,000
SUBSCRIBERS
MILESTONE
Apr 29, 2023
Giulia Segreti

How Are Erotic Readings born?

All this comes from the strong passion for acting and books.

I still love to interpret and try my hand at totally different songs.

In addition to romantic and erotic scenes, I also engage in action and adrenaline-charged ones.

I wanted to bring a new audio book idea and so I did!

The usual audio books are flat, monotonous and hasty with even a single voice.

I have combined acting and dubbing, creating something exciting, different and true.

And this is how Giulia Segreti's " READING FILMS " were born.

My key is acting.

Try as much as possible to convey the feeling and mood of the protagonist.

" I feel them while I play and it's a beautiful and indescribable feeling. "

It is like being estranged from reality and then being catapulted into a different world, into a different story, where you are no longer you but take on the appearance of another.

You are another person.

You think like her.

Yes I know, it is difficult to explain and understand it.

It's pure madness .... pure magic.

My Audioleggi are followed and this is a great pleasure for us.

I also receive messages from people who come back tired from work or school, have a good time relaxing listening to us.

We always thank you for the positive comments you make us every time we upload something. And one thank you is actually very little. It is as if we have known each other for a long time.

It is since 2012, when I opened my YouTube channel, that you support us :) We have established a virtual friendship relationship with you. Because every time a new reading of a 'film' that is about to come out is in the works, we 'sclerot' together about possible scenes. In fact, I also receive messages of the type " thanks to you, the release of the film is less nerve-wracking and you make us dream with scenes that we will not see in the film ".

We will always be grateful to you audience for your affection. By now I have grown fond of each of you and I will not forget anything.

I met some of you live and hugged them tightly.

You rocked me with your precious drawings, even letters that you dedicated to us and much more !!

THANK YOU

How do I choose erotic readings?

First, I choose the most important and significant parts.

I especially prefer parts of dialogue and in fact the narrated part is cut. We often change the parts also to have a cinematic effect. Some of the comments I get are " but is the film out? " Or " where can I find the film? "

In reality, the film does not exist and the peculiarity is to transform just a simple reading into a film!

After choosing the piece, you register!

It also happens that a kiss is described in the piece.

What do I do in these cases?

Well, to make everything more real and similar to a movie, we reproduce the verses and kisses directly ourselves. So the kisses you feel on some readings are REAL! As well as the spanking that we have reproduced in various Erotic readings.

Then the challenging part is up to the assembly.

It depends on the length of the piece.

Then sound effects, music, voices, effects, echoes in the thoughts of the characters, 3D audio etc ... are fixed.

Sometimes I insert some Cover Recited in Italian by me.

To better understand what they are, you can find them in my main YouTube channel or in my 3rd YouTube channel called:

"Giulia Segreti Music"

Binaural 3d Audio

In some readings you will find another peculiarity '.

What's this?

It is a three-dimensional sound recording that has the purpose of optimizing the audio for listening with headphones, reproducing the acoustic perceptions of a listener located in the original environment where the sound event was recorded.

You need to have excellent earphones, always keep your head straight vertically while listening and CLOSE YOUR EYES.

And we also have binaural sound effect movie readings!

Nothing is missing :)

We also started at a time when audio books were not known and there was no insane competition like now.

But the public is always faithful and then our readings do not last for many hours, precisely because, thanks to some research we have done, our average public does not have much free time. They have been designed to last 5/10 minutes or a little more.

In fact, the short videos are the most viewed.

We interpret unpublished FANFICTION written by Fans such as the fanfiction on LUCIFER written by the talented Arianna Muscio! You can find them all in my channel!

Erotic Audioreader

The term " erotic audiologist " is the result of second thoughts and various tests.

The TV appreciated this detail of mine and so I wanted to exaggerate it and adapt it to the very popular Trash world.

Then this nickname gets closer and closer to me, placing me in a special sector in the vein of EROTIC READINGS.

Then managing to be the first and only one who interprets hot Italian novels in an exaggeratedly erotic way!

Then the difficulty in the world of social media lies precisely in inventing and bringing to light originality.

I often invent stories or carry over the daily sex life of several people who send me their private writings, and then upload them to YouTube.

Example of Erotic Audioreading

The Time

The time it takes to prepare a reading is about 2 hours but it depends on various factors:

- ➔ LENGTH OF READING
- ➔ CHOICE OF HISTORY
- ➔ TRANSLATION
- ➔ SOUND EFFECTS
- ➔ MUSIC

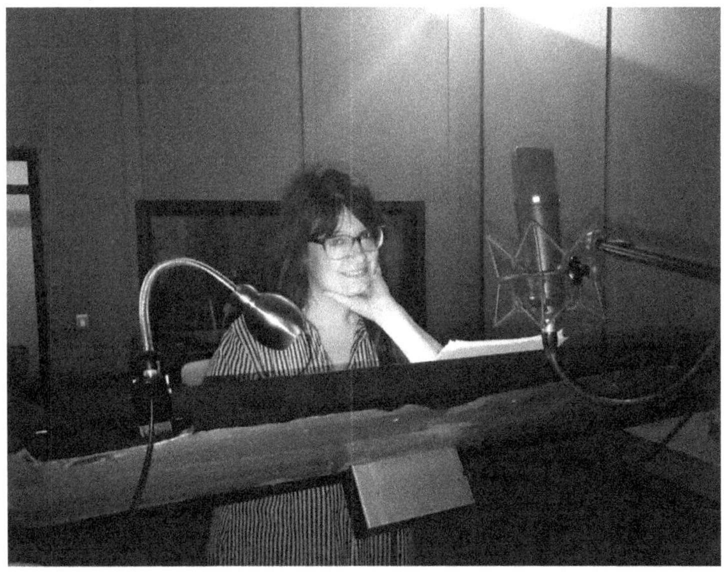

The Foreign public

Many of my videos have been translated into many languages.

You can notice this peculiarity in my youtube video by clicking on " CC " which will activate the translated subtitles.

And everything is automatically translated by youtube.

This has helped our popularity to foreign audiences.

We are delighted with this opportunity that has been granted to us.

You will also find some readings recited by us in English !!

Barone Mark Kheel

His nickname B.M.K. , acronym of BARONE MARK KHEEL, derives from his passion for anime he had had since the age of 10.

In particular, for the anime " DEATH NOTE ", according to her, her first animated masterpiece seen on TV in which her favorite character

" MELLO " reveals her real name " MIHAEL KEEHL ".

Here is how he invented his stage name at the time:

- " MIHAEL " became " MARK " from Marco.

- " KHEEL " underwent Englishization by moving the letter " H " to second place.

- " BARONE " was added a few years later to give a tone of Elegance and improve its pronunciation!

In short, if you don't know how to look for an art name ...

he'll take care of it !!

Your novel as if it were a film

We also produce Audiobooks and Audioreadings on commission for writers and writers! There are several packages you can choose!

HOW DOES IT WORK?

We create complete Audiobooks or short Audioreadings on commission with our voices! You can choose the music, sound effects etc.…

The author can choose the piece we have to interpret and also the duration!

WHERE CAN YOU CONTACT US?

For more information, also for other types of advertising that we create, write here:

EMAIL: **giuliasegretiauthor@gmail.com**

Please add **THIS CODE** in the email to get the 20% discount.

CODICE: GIULIA20

*** **For those who buy the PAPER copy, it has**

1 FREE READ of 2 PAGES*

Be born on YouTube

YouTube is the most used video sharing platform in the world, it allows you to watch videos and listen to music.

Whose idea was it?

Jawed Karim posted the first video on YouTube.

Eighteen seconds in which he is seen with his back to an elephant cage and shows what he is visiting on vacation to his family.

His idea was to share a video to show it to multiple relatives, instead of sending it one by one.

It was the first video uploaded to YouTube, the first user to register as a YouTube channel, but also the founder together with

Chad Hurley and Steve Chen.

A year later YouTube is already a giant of the web

This growth attracts Google owners. It will be the owners of Google who will acquire YouTube.

On YouTube, master creativity and talent.

Talent can also be that of sharing and changing various strategies at the right time.

YouTube rewards originality!

Unfortunately, time is the solution.

A video can go viral even after a year.

Only after you have met the requirements for monetization, have you passed the first goal.

The important is:

-be creative and unique

- do not copy other people's video styles

- have a lot of patience

- sharing

- be ready for anything, even for any letters from courts etc ...

Life on YouTube is not easy:

you have to be ready for anything. Both positive and negative things.

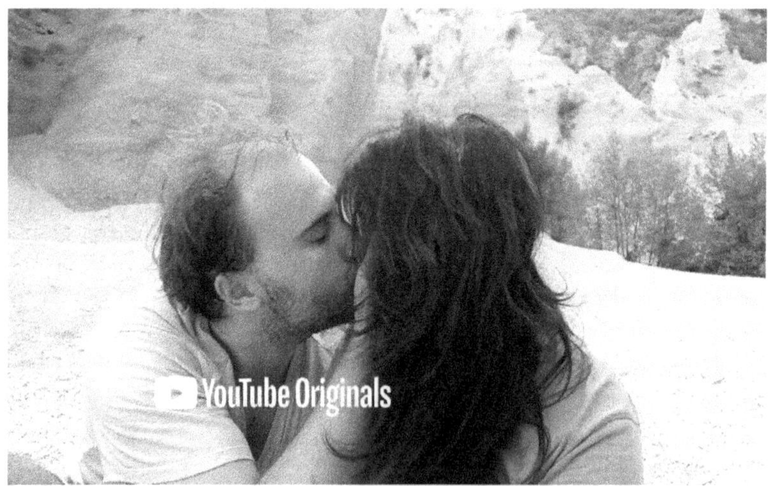

G.Segreti e B.M.K. - LAME ROSSE – Fiastra

My cover recited

I also dedicate myself to the COVER RECITED in Italian. It is a very special genre. They are covers sung and acted at the same time.

You can find them in my 1st and 3rd YouTube channel!

3rd channel: GIULIA SECRETI MUSIC

I wait for you! Sign up there too !!

Motivational audio and Asmr

We are giving life to other innovations such as

MOTIVATIONAL AUDIO AND ASMR:

• For erotic relaxation for him and for her [ASMR]

• As an exhortation to face life in a positive way with quotes and monologues from FILMS and SERIES [Motivational Audio]

YouTube Shorts

Let's not forget the SHORTS that I always make on my main channel.

They are short videos lasting a few seconds that are very popular in the United States.

I have created real whatsapp chats relating to famous couples in the movies!

2° YouTube Channel

Instead in my 2nd YouTube channel you will find only and exclusively all the Italian readings of emerging writers!

And for those who make film readings with us, they will also have 'this 2nd channel available for advertising'!

You can find it on YouTube as:

GIULIA SEGRETI EXTRA

Your novel as if it were a film…

We also produce audiobooks and audio-readings on commission for writers and writers! There are several packages you can choose from!

HOW DOES IT WORK?

We make complete or short audio books on commission with our voices!

You can choose the music, sound effects etc.…

The author can choose the piece we have to interpret and also the duration!

WHERE CAN YOU CONTACT US?

For more information, also for other types of advertising we produce, write here:

EMAIL: **giuliasegretiauthor@gmail.com**

Please write me **THIS CODE** to get a 20% discount

CODE: GIULIA20

Theater

Before being Audiolectors, one must also be an actor.

The more talent and predisposition you have for this discipline [acting], the more you perceive the passion and the way in which you are able to excite the hearts of the listeners.

I have played several roles in the theater.

Miss Lynch in Grease, Cleante in Moliere's L'Avaro, Titania in A Midsummer Night's Dream etc ....

On the beach, at the theater, in the wine shop etc ...

Playing a young boy in Moliere's L'Avaro was fun and very difficult at the same time!

I also make FX Masks and FX special effects such as the beard that I created myself to play the male role in L'Avaro :)

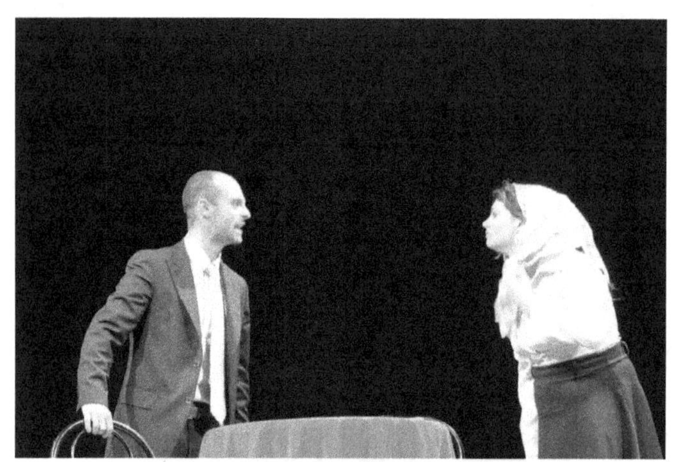

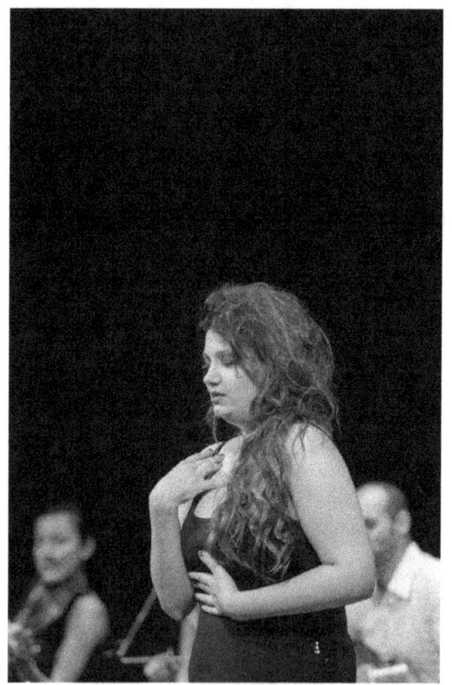

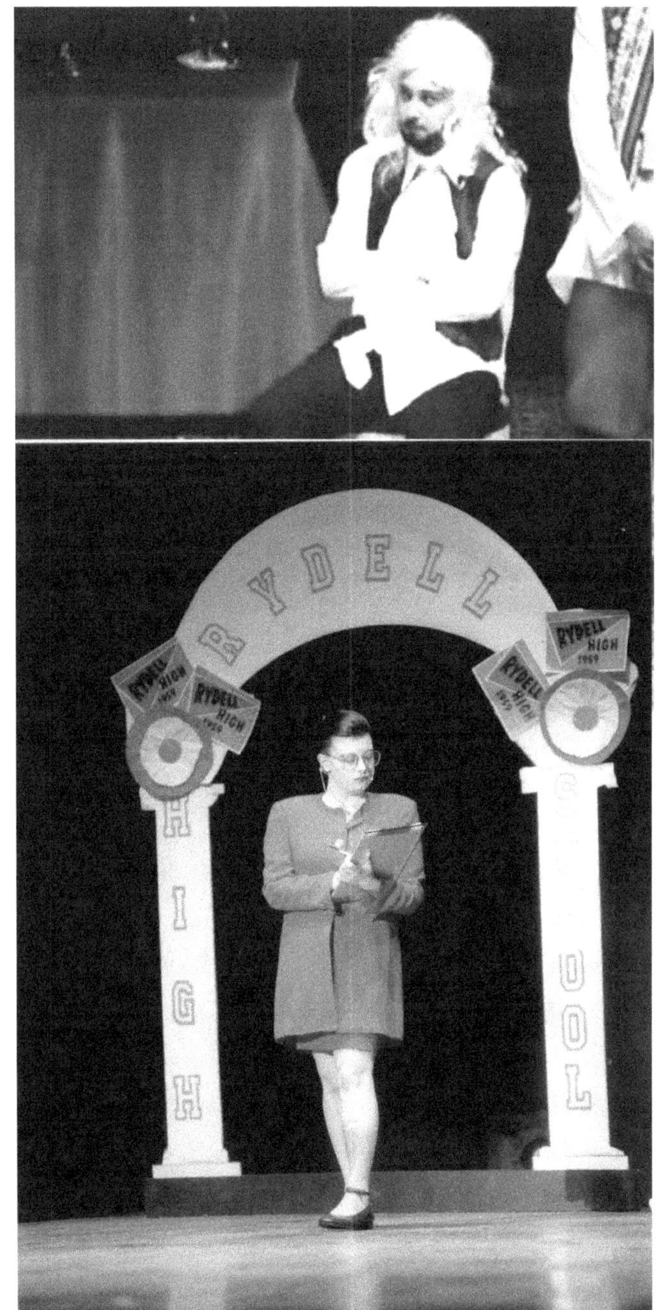

RYDELL
HIGH
RYDELL HIGH 1959
RYDELL HIGH 1959
RYDELL HIGH 1959
RYDELL HIGH 1959
H
I
G
H
O
O
L

We have participated as COSPLAYERS at the Rome Comics Fair several times.

The first year, in 2014, as cosplayers of the SHADOWHUNTERS couple.

Later as AUGUSTUS and HAZEL of GUILT OF THE STARS and ... believe me ... we had many details, even the novel by Peter Van Houten created by me !! What good memories! Many people stopped us to take a picture!

Finally we returned as a couple 50 SHADES dressed as Anastasia and Christian Gray!

THEN ONE OF OUR DREAMS HAS COME TRUE !!

Thanks to our YouTube channels, we were hosted by the Fair and we went on the big stage of youtubers to present our voices and EROTIC readings !!

Pavilion 6 of the Youtubers !!

We were presented with a beautiful Trailer!

[you can see it on my YouTube channel or at the end of each reading]

We are satisfied with this milestone.

PARTICIPATE IN THE CONTEST
YOUR MINI EROTIC STORY
IT COMES TO LIFE

In this book you will also find several competitions!

What is it about? How does it work??

TELL us briefly about a personal or invented erotic night.

The most important things are your emotions, your memories and even a pinch of imagination :)

Once you have completed the erotic mini story...SEND IT TO ME!

Email: **giuliasegretiauthor@gmail.com**

Write in the SUBJECT section: Mini Erotic Story

Don't forget to write your first and last name

[also a pseudonym]

and LINK of the instagram profile!!

the story must be exactly 1 page long

It will be uploaded to the GIULIA SEGRETI YOUTUBE CHANNEL

My poems

One of the most famous and important texts written and interpreted by me is:

I dedicated this post to my partner " BMK "

for our anniversary!

A beautiful and short dedication full of love and passion.

I uploaded it to FB to surprise my love and in the following days it reached 6,000,000 views and became one of the most viral romantic videos on the web!

Unfortunately, many Facebook, Instagram and several FanEditor pages stole the video or audio [even more serious] without mentioning me.

I managed to close these pages but unfortunately someone new always comes out ...

I REMIND YOU THAT YOU FIND THIS TEXT INTERPRETED BY ME IN MY YOUTUBE CHANNEL, PAGE AND FACEBOOK PROFILE!

There is also a passage I wrote that refers to us, our voices and the dubbing of the READINGS! And few have really understood its meaning;)

TRUE LOVE
[Eng Version]

Love should be considered as the most beautiful feeling ever, even if many times it is considered the opposite…

perhaps because it is what makes us suffer the most.

Love is part of the heart, it cannot be controlled, manipulated… it cannot be anything but love.

Love for family, country, friends.

Even if, when it comes to love, each of us thinks of that he or that she would like to have next to us.

Love is part of our days, but what is it that makes it special?

Maybe being able to look him in the eye and not need anything else.

Maybe it's loving who you've always loved even after you've lost them.

Perhaps that feeling that makes us feel good when you know you are the first thought of him makes it special.

Or maybe... it's understanding that you didn't suffer unnecessarily when, after so many tears, he's next to you again.

And then you understand that true love never ends.

Love is madness.

Love is dying at the mere thought that another can take his place.

Love is that feeling that makes us feel at peace with the whole world.

That, even if it collapsed, you wouldn't give a damn because it's your world.

True Love is when a person enters your deepest intimate sphere, so much so that you feel they are an integral part not only of your soul but also of your body.

Finding a part of yourself in the other, so much so that you can't do without it.

Enough to feel torn, massacred, incomplete if the other is no longer there.

It is something so powerful and strong that there are no difficulties and quarrels.

Now my other side lives with me every moment of my life, shares every joy and every pain with me.

He is constantly close to me.

It is the first thought in the morning and the last in the evening.

Populate my dreams and my anxieties.

Now I'm sure, in life you really love only once

The energy of true love is too intense to be able to share it with more people.

And on the other hand Plato explained that:

"There is one and only other part of you in the universe."

With him I would now run away from everything and everyone.

I want to be with him.

Hug him, kiss him and live him every second of my life.

Please take me away!

Almost always, we abandon our bodies to give voice to others...but coincidentally...I always fall in love with the same person.***

I know you will take care of me and defend me with your heart.

I love you! And you know it.

This great love will live in me forever as long as I live.

True love exists.

And now you give me a kiss?

GIULIA SEGRETI

*Meanings and curiosities****

The first sentence "Almost always, we abandon our bodies to give voice to others...but coincidentally...I always fall in love with the same person"

it refers to the two of us interpreting the readings, voicing the characters and in fact abandoning our bodies to step into the shoes of the characters in the books or films.

Instead for the phrase "And now you give me a kiss?" the meaning is different.

It was our anniversary and as a gift I created this poem dedicated to him and later dubbed it. Once finished, I saved the video in a usb stick. The same evening I show him the video and the last sentence, a question, is addressed to him who was sitting on the sofa. If he could give me a kiss as a " reward " for creating this wonderful video and audio :) and so it happened.

USE THE QR CODE TO LISTEN TO THE VIDEOPOETRY!

Tv and radio!

I conducted a local radio and I was interviewed on Radio Serena, RDS, Radio Italia 60s, RLB, Suprime, FROGS and many other radios !!

We also appeared on TV to show our Erotic Audio Readings! We try to aim higher and higher :)

You can find me in the credits of an episode of EMIGRATIS of the third edition which is entitled " Che Bello " and I thank Pio and Amedeo! It was also a strong emotion because they contacted me and followed new fans on Instagram.

Then to AVANTI ANOTHER my boyfriend participated as a competitor and I was lucky enough to meet Paolo Bonolis and Luca Laurenti and to go on stage, then interpreting an erotic reading of 50 Shades.

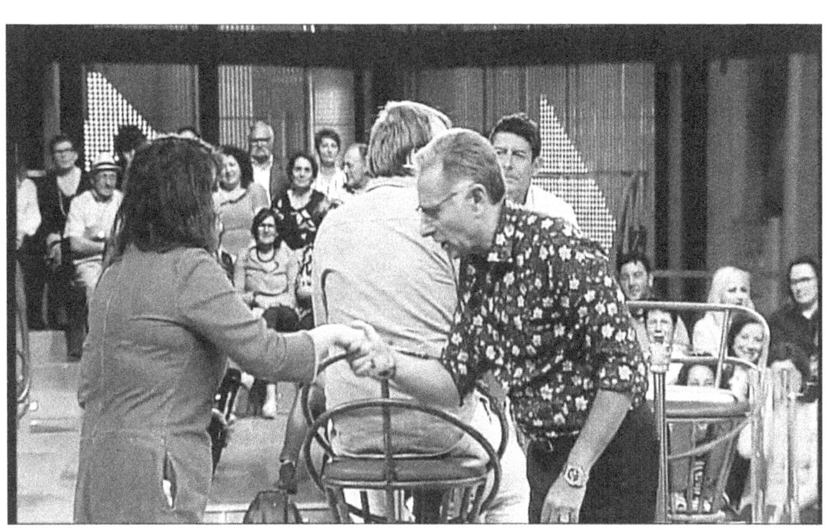

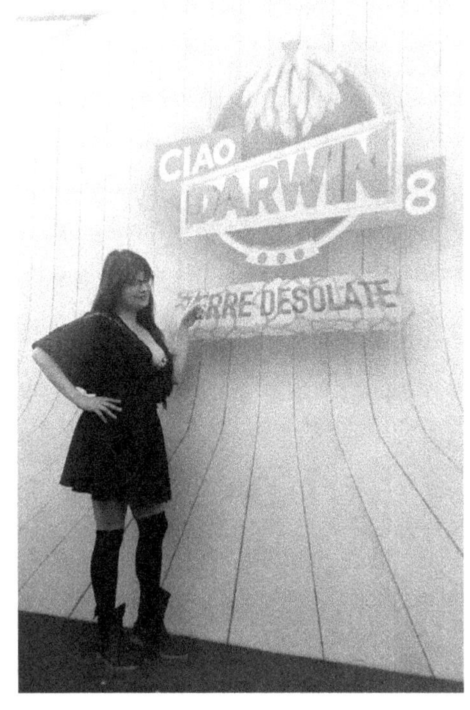
CIAO
DARWIN 8
TERRE DESOLATE

Happiness skyrockets also with my entry to CIAO DARWIN 8 obviously in the category of "Messaline".

As a little girl I used to watch this program together with dad Manlio and how many laughs we had. And then being there on the steps of Ciao Darwin was a great emotion and for me it had a double meaning.

I hope I managed to get a smile out of my father who looks at me from up there.

Interview

As always, I thank the Bloggers, the newspapers and all those who have dedicated a beautiful space to us with beautiful interviews and super curious questions. Here are some of these questions to get to know us better.

The Giulia Segreti YouTube channel boasts over 65,000 subscribers and there are more than 40,000 "likes" on the Facebook page of the same name. Would you like to tell us how your adventure was born and how it grew?

Barone: Before knowing each other, Giulia and I were part of a Facebook group of Italian amateur voice actors and one day I saw the announcement of Giulia who was looking for a male voice for a character from her audio-readings, so I proposed myself and from that moment on we have started to develop and expand this beautiful idea, dealing with several books and also helping with translations from English when it was necessary to dub a clip. It is only thanks to her that I got to know this fantastic world of audio-reading because I didn't even know what it was before. From that first collaboration of ours, in which we also discovered that we were neighbors from the city, we began to collaborate and feel more and more and in the end we fell in love. We have been together for over 6 years now.

Giulia: All for fun and passion. Barone has revealed to you more or less how we met, but my growth, which then became "ours", I think started from the first Shadowhunters reading I uploaded. I noticed that people liked it a lot and we never stopped from there. I contacted Barone because I found him great for the role of Jace Wayland and believe me ... the other guys I evaluated and heard weren't capable at all. Even if, I repeat, I wasn't all this summit either, and I never will be, because we all make some mistakes anyway.

[LIBEROVOLO]

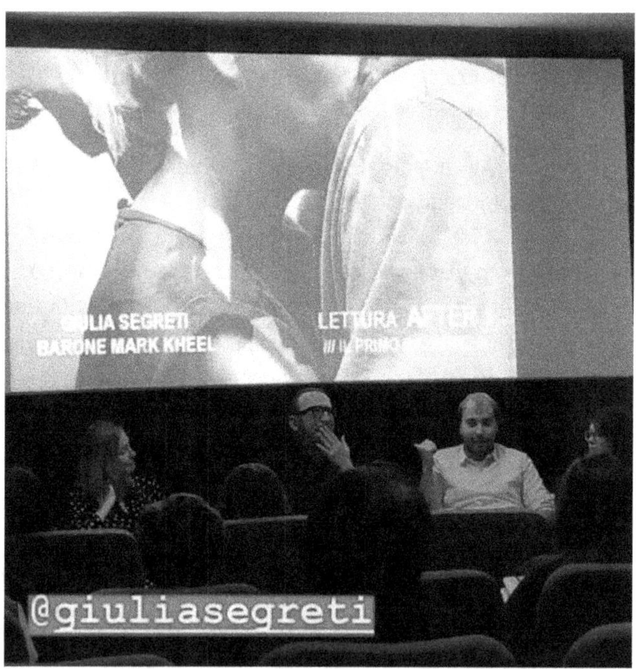

CASA DEL CINEMA, ROME.

How did you find yourself in this somewhat "erotic" role?

I love it, especially the book. Seduction through the voice is a new thing that I have experienced …

[VOCI.FM]

Giulia and Marco companions on the web and in life, are super loved by the people of the network for the Fan Made trailers. It involves creating a video in the form of a trailer that will serve as a launch for an audio-reading based on a particular novel, this video introduces images from famous films or TV series, whose protagonists take on the role of the main actors of the audio-reading.

In Giulia's channel, the absolute protagonist is the voice and it's like seeing a movie with your eyes closed... we just need to listen.

Among the audio-readings in Giulia's channel, which have met with great success, we find the EROTIC READINGS …

… While among the Fan Made trailers recently made with Barone we find that of "After", taken from the bestseller by Anna Todd, which to date has exceeded 4 million views.

Not only the web, but also television is beginning to appreciate the two youtubers.

In fact, in 2018, after passing an audition, they dubbed some lines of the first episode of X Factor and a few days ago they appeared in the famous program "Avanti un Altro", hosted by Paolo Bonolis. Who knows what's cooking!

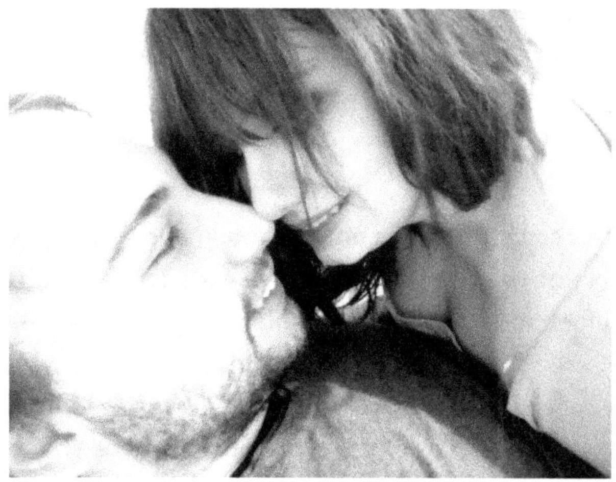

Welcome Giulia, what relationship do you have with the romance genre?

Thanks for the invitation, I have a wonderful relationship with the romance genre because since I started reading and "hearing" this kind of books I have never stopped and today I have been able to build an identity on them.

As an audio reader, which audio-reading appealed to you the most and why?

Absolutely those of the 50 Shades saga because in them I was able to find many themes and aspects wonderfully mixed to create a wonderful story.

[SINS OF PEN]

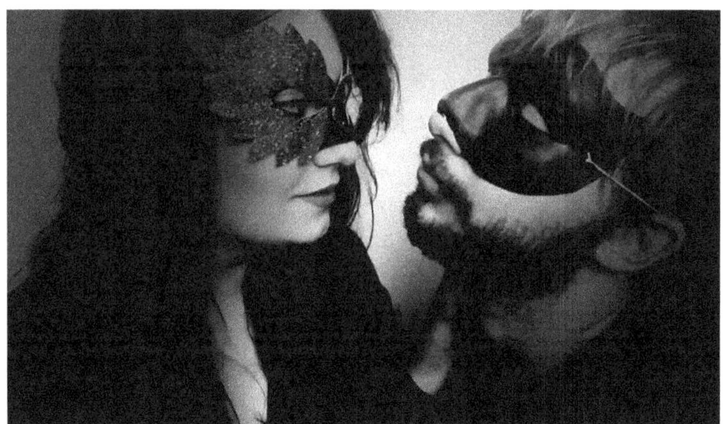

Did you do special studies to learn how to dub or are you self-taught?

I started doing short voice exercises with very few instruments (I was recording with an older generation cellphone): I also noticed that my voice was very different recorded and I hated it very much. Unfortunately, I didn't have anyone in my family who could help me out or understand if I was capable or not, so I started as self-taught. Dubbing accompanied me throughout my adolescence, then the voice changed with age and I discovered new tones. As soon as I finished high school my mother gave me a dubbing course in Rome which I concluded with good grades.

[GREATERFOOL.TV]

 Tell us a little about your work as an actress, voice actress and audio player.

I have been doing theater for several years, even playing the part of a man! And to think as such, on stage in the theater. Yes, it's crazy and very difficult! But I have learned so many things. I was also Miss Lynch in Grease so I had to play the role of a woman of a certain age. In short, all roles that were detached from my age and my sex.

Then it was also the moment of a character that I loved a lot. Titania in A Midsummer Night's Dream. Seductive but also treacherous for a few moments. For audio readings, after the success of 50 Shades, I'm finishing AFTER….

We also make audiobooks and audio-readings on commission for many female writers. Now I'm in talks with "Audible" to release an entire audiobook made with our voices. In the dubbing, on the other hand, I gave voice to the character of TAYLOR METTERNICH in the movie "TUO SIMON" and ELEVEN in the TV movie "THE ARCHER". I then dubbed other roles in films such as "DEGREESE OF FEAR" and "NIGHTMARE MOM". I really miss trying cartoons, while my boyfriend, Baron Mark Kheel, lent his voice to the cartoon "ZOMBILLENIUM" and to the protagonist Reid in the movie "MY NAME IS FEARLESS" aired on Netflix. In short, we are slowly doing something. Finally, my boyfriend and I are also Official VOICES of the X FACTOR ITALIA 2018 theme song - Auditions.

[SIMPLY FRIENDLY]

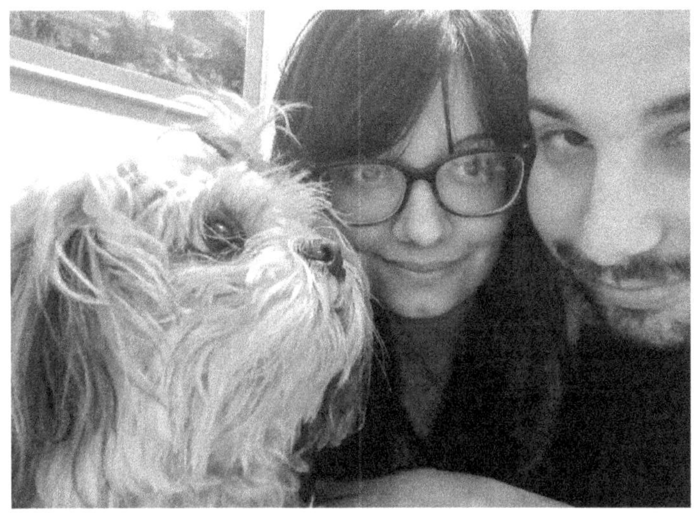

WHERE TO FIND US

Our Socials

-YOUTUBE   @giuliasegreti

-FACEBOOK   @giuliasegreti   @baronemarkkheel

-FACEBOOK PAGE   @giuliasegreti   @BMK's Room

-INSTAGRAM   @giuliasegreti   @baronemarkkheel

-TIKTOK   @giuliasegreti

QR CODE YOUTUBE ''GIULIA SEGRETI''

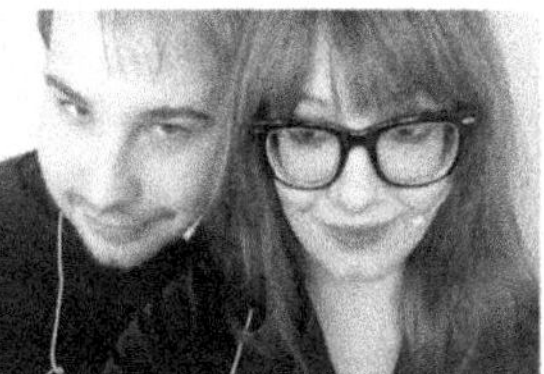
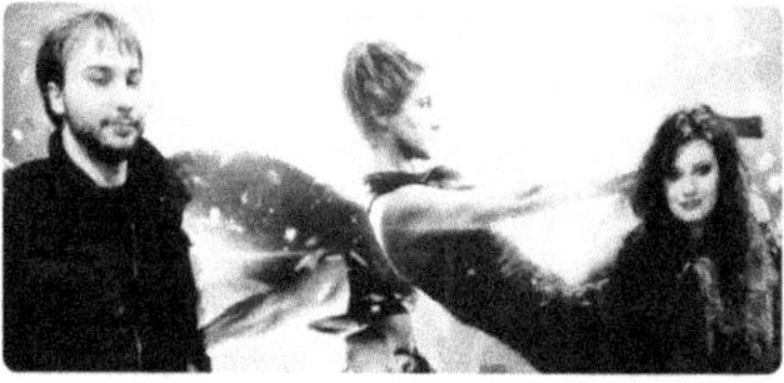

Giulia e Marco famosi su You Tube **con le audioletture, il canale ha 9 mln di visualizzazioni**

Quando la voce diventa protagonista

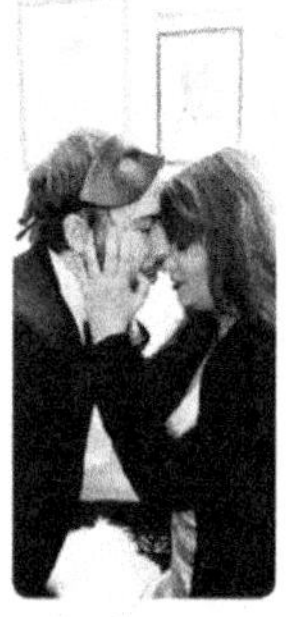
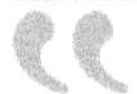

I DUE FERMANI, ATTORI E DOPPIATORI, GRAZIE A TALENTO, EFFETTI SONORI E MUSICA ANIMANO I LIBRI CULT

di Alessandra Bruno

L'emozione ha voce. Soprattutto se ad animare le parole ci pensano Giulia Segreti e Marco Cognigni, in arte Barone Mark Kheel. I due giovani del Fermano, 25 anni lei, 24 lui, grazie al loro talento sono diventati famosi sul web. Audiolettori, attori e doppiatori, hanno unito l'amore per i libri e quello per il mondo del cinema. Le loro letture magiche trasformano in realtà fiumi di parole: «E' come guardare un film ad occhi chiusi», dicono. La formula è piaciuta ai fan, il successo è nato a colpi di clic. In tre anni il canale su You Tube(Giulia Segreti), aperto nel febbraio 2014, ha raggiunto 9 milioni di visualizzazioni e conta ben 22 mila iscritti. Su Fb, invece, i fan sono schizzati a quota 11 mila. Giulia, a Roma, ha frequentato la scuola di doppiaggio di Roberto Chevalier, voce ufficiale di Tom Cruise, e entrambi hanno seguito il corso di teatro di Stefano Tosoni a Porto San Giorgio, per perfezionare la loro esperienza. La coppia, tra un'interpretazione e l'altra, si è perfino innamorata: «Tutto è nato con la prima lettura- confida Marco- quella della saga urban fantasy "Shadowhunters"; lei cercava una voce maschile e ha pubblicato l'annuncio in una chat sui social dedicata ai doppiatori. Io sono stato il primo a rispondere. Poi, dopo sei mesi, ci siamo fidanzati». «L'avevo già notato- precisa Giulia- trovavo la sua voce bellissima». E il feeling si sente. Letteralmente. I giovani hanno interpretato, tra gli altri, "Io Prima di te", "Colpa delle stelle", "Hunger games", "After" e il fantasy "Divergent". A far breccia nel cuore degli utenti, però, sono state le pagine prese in prestito alla trilogia cult "Cinquanta sfumature": «Il commento più bello che abbiamo ricevuto? A qualcuno è piaciuto più ascoltarci che vedere il film. Forse per la qualità del doppiaggio in italiano, forse per le parti del libro sacrificate. Chissà. Comunque ne siamo onorati». L'idea di aprire un canale è nata per caso, ma le premesse erano buone: «A 13 anni - racconta Giulia- ho cominciato con i primi doppiaggi in camera mia, con mezzi più rudimentali. Usavo il cellulare invece che il microfono per registrare la mia voce». Oggi casa di Giulia è diventata uno studio di registrazione con tutte le attrezzature professionali. Microfoni, effetti sonori, audio speciale in 3D e musica, fanno la differenza: «Di solito le audio letture risultano un po' piatte - conferma la coppia- a noi piace che le parole fuoriescano veramente dal libro. Usiamo anche alcune tecniche per rendere tutto più fedele, come il battito delle mani o lo schiocco di un bacio quando vengono descritti». La narrazione che accarezza l'udito, può essere una coccola per l'anima: «Non ci avevamo pensato - ammette Marco- ma ci hanno scritto genitori e parenti di persone che hanno problemi di dislessia o di vista. Ci hanno ringraziato e noi ci siamo commossi». Giulia nel 2014 è stata premiata come "miglior voce" dal doppiatore Teo Bellia.

La coppia ha interpretato diverse letture del libro "703 ragioni per dire sì" della scrittrice L.F. Kotaline, doppiato la serie tv "Colorina" in onda su SoS Tv ed è apparsa anche nell'edizione Tg5 all'interno di una clip del film "Io Prima di te". Il sogno? «Doppiare il nostro primo film». ●

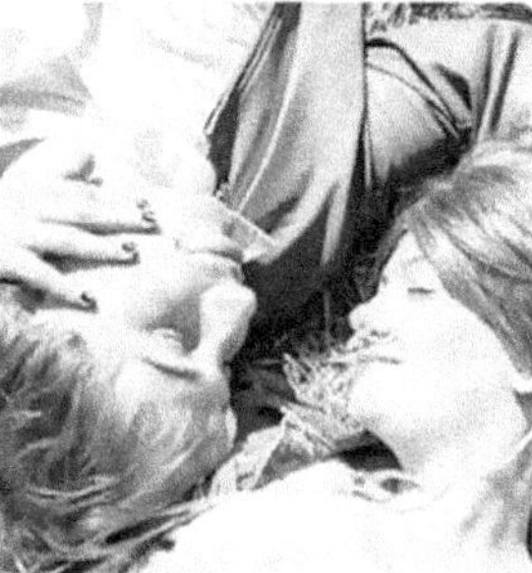
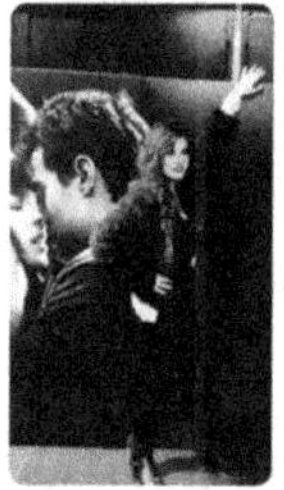
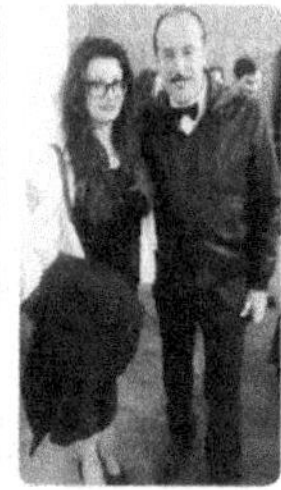
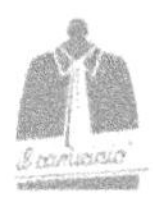

Ogni lettura è come guardare un film ad occhi chiusi. In futuro? Vorremmo doppiarne uno al cinema

Nelle immagini Giulia Segreti e Marco Cognigni i due audiolettori famosi su You Tube. A destra, Giulia con Lopez

THE AUDIOBOOKS THAT WE MADE WITH OUR VOICES

We take care of the creation of complete audiobooks on commission, always maintaining our style.

These are the ones we have achieved so far.

You can find them on my YouTube channel and on AUDIBLE.

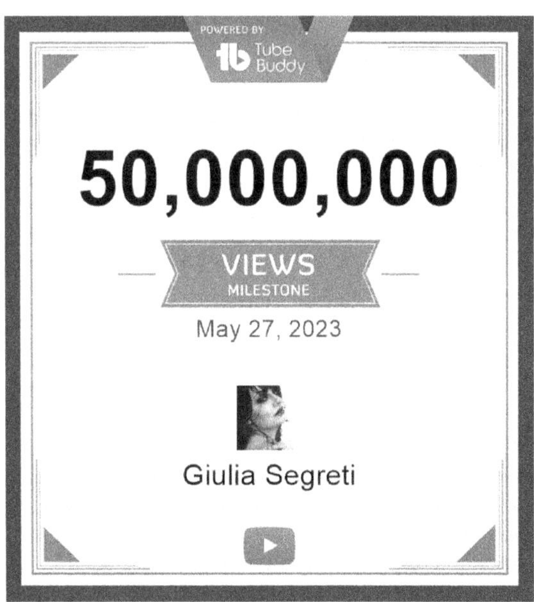

THE AUDIO-READINGS...

OF ITALIAN WRITERS

In my Youtube channel, you will also find many audio readings that we create for emerging and non-emerging Italian writers and writers.

I'm so happy to introduce you to new genres with our voices.

Below is the complete list of all movie readings that are available in my channel.

Are you curious and haven't listened to this very hot read yet?? No problem :)

After seeing the list, paste the title of the novel accompanied by my name and surname into the YouTube search string.

Example: **<u>YOUR FAULT</u> Giulia Segreti**

And the game is done, the reading link will appear immediately :)

Happy erotic listening!!!

I also remind you that in the description and in the comments of the video reading on YouTube you will always find the plot and the purchase link on Amazon for ebook and paper format!

LIST OF AUDIO READINGS

BY ITALIAN AUTHORS

Here, on the other hand, is the list of readings of Italian novels that you can find on my YouTube channel. Surely I have forgotten some writers, but you will find the PLAYLIST 'SELF-CE AUTHOR BOOKS' complete with 250 readings!

CONTINUE HERE.

OF 300 READINGS

After: Hero & Anna Todd
and i meet my fans

Rome.

Another great indescribable emotion.

For the first time in my life I met and embraced the actor and author of AFTER.

HERO FIENNES TIFFIN

ANNA TODD

I remember when my love for a birthday present presented me with the complete collection of the 5 AFTER books edited by Sperling Kupfer.

I didn't know After and from here I started with the audio readings!

After our success, I had the honor of meeting and getting to know them.

Thanks to Leone Film Group and TW.

On the same day, the actor and the writer went to the bookstore to sign copies.

After a few hours we went out of the bookstore and the surprise came from you fans. You recognized us and we hugged each other.

In your After novels there are also our signatures and for us this is a beautiful gift.

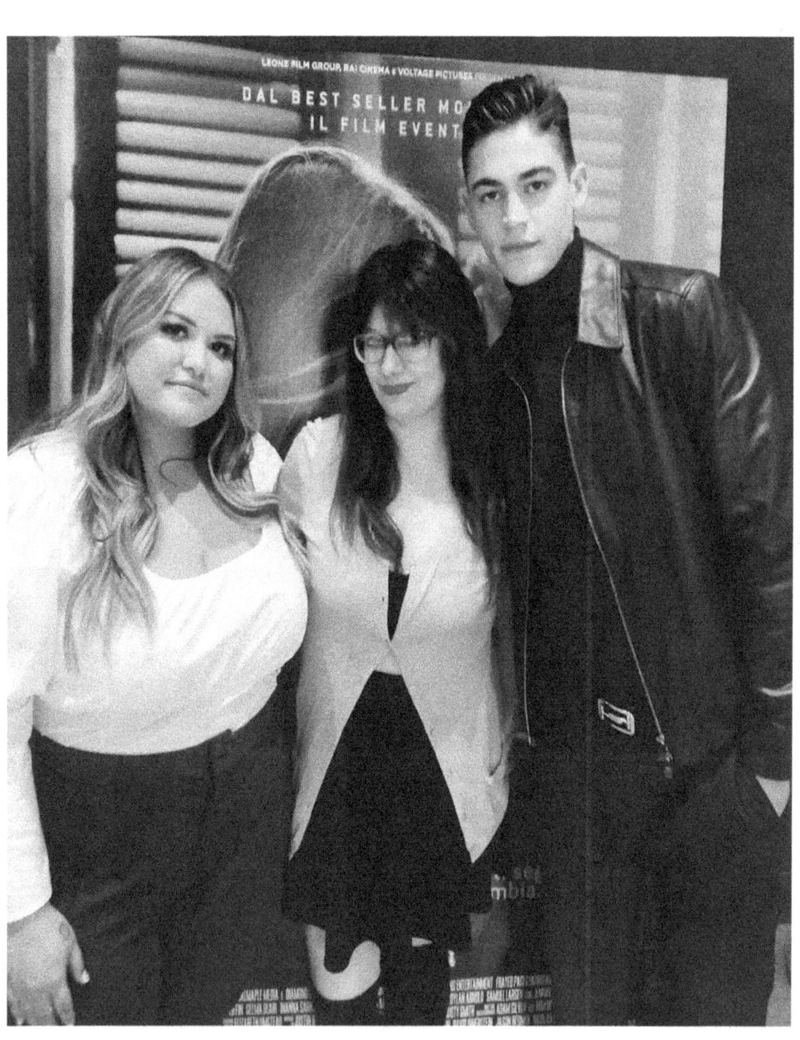

LEONE FILM GROUP, RAI CINEMA e VOLTAGE PICTURES
DAL BEST SELLER MO
IL FILM EVENT

PARTICIPATE IN THE CONTEST

WHATSAPP MESSAGES

In this book you will also find several competitions!

What is it about? How does it work??

Write at least 6 lines of invented Whatsapp dialogue of a famous couple taken from books and films such as "AFTER: Hardin and Tessa" or "50 Shades: Christian and Anastasia".

EXAMPLE:

-What are you doing Tessa?

-I'm going to take a shower, are you coming with me?

Once completed...SEND IT TO ME!

Email: **giuliasegretiauthor@gmail.com**

Write in the SUBJECT section: Whatsapp Chat

Don't forget to write your name and surname in the email

[also a pseudonym]

and the LINK of the Instagram profile!!

It will be uploaded to the GIULIA SEGRETI YOUTUBE CHANNEL

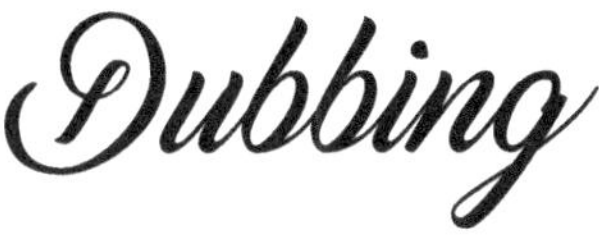

Dubbing

We have both dubbed several films, TV series and cartoons in Rome and Milan.

We are happy to have voiced Tales for Children in the studio and Baron voiced the protagonist in the Netflix cartoon " My Name Is' Fearless' ', vocally playing the role of Reid.

We recently teamed up with director Gustavo Garrafa on his cartoon PLUSH PUPPIES which ended up on AMAZON PRIME!

We previously had the honor of voicing the second season of the TV series " COLUMNS " with him.

I voiced Taylor Metternich in the movie 'Your Simon' and I am featured in other films such as 'Enemy Mothers', 'The Archer' etc ....

Biography

Giulia Segreti was born on January 6, 1992 in Fermo and lives in Torre San Patrizio with her partner. He studied acting for 4 years and attended a dubbing course in Rome. In 2012 she opened her YouTube channel.

Marco Cognigni was born in Ancona on 11 July 1993. He graduated from the faculty of mathematics and applications in Camerino and currently teaches in several high schools. Since 2014 he has collaborated with Giulia Segreti in the creation of audio-readings and dubbing on YouTube

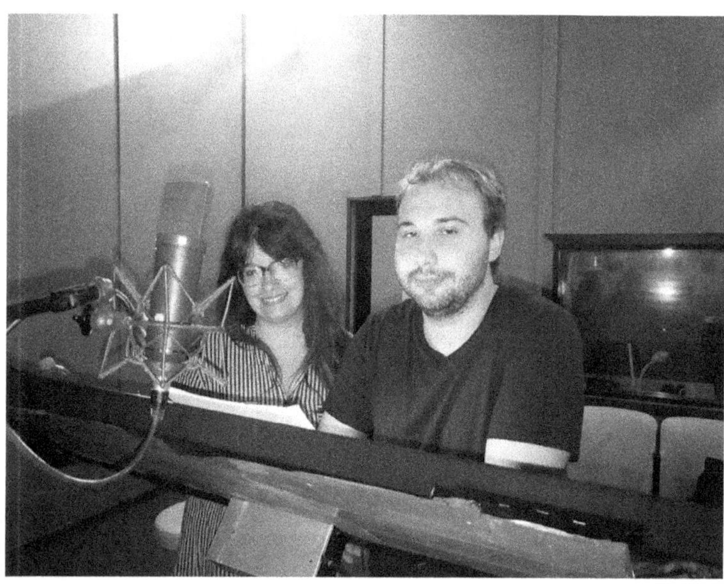

Thanks to

Thanks to my love and colleague Barone Mark Kheel for supporting me in making this book and others to come very soon! Thanks because you are always with me! Thanks also for having me as editor and proofreader.

I love you!

Thanks to all our Italian writers :) I hope this book is another way to make you known !!

Then I thank all those who follow us and the newcomers!

We hope, with our voices, to make you experience beautiful erotic emotions and more;)

I'm waiting for you on my Youtube and Instagram channel " GIULIA SEGRETI "

YOUTUBE CHANNEL GIULIA SEGRETI

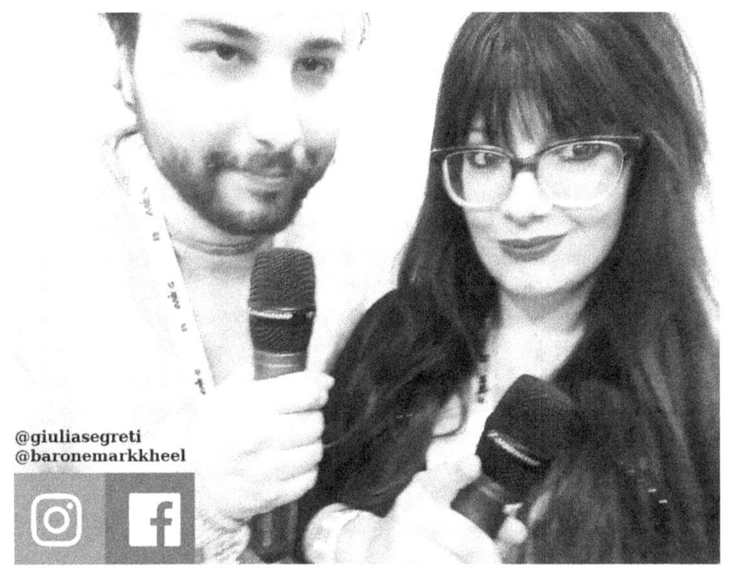

@giuliasegreti
@baronemarkkheel

ROMICS [Rome]

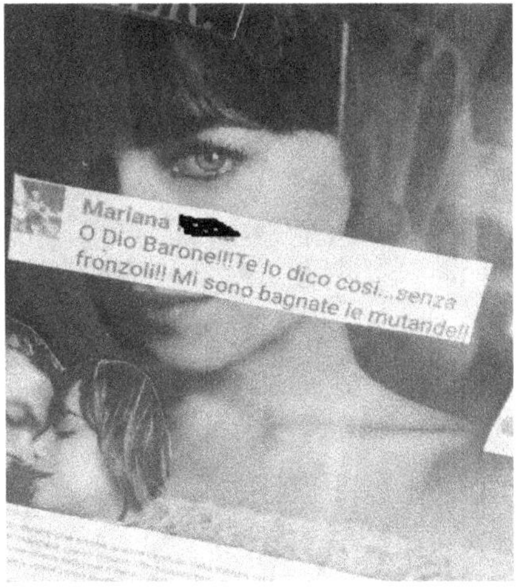

Mariana
O Dio Barone!!!Te lo dico così...senza
fronzoli!! Mi sono bagnate le mutande!!

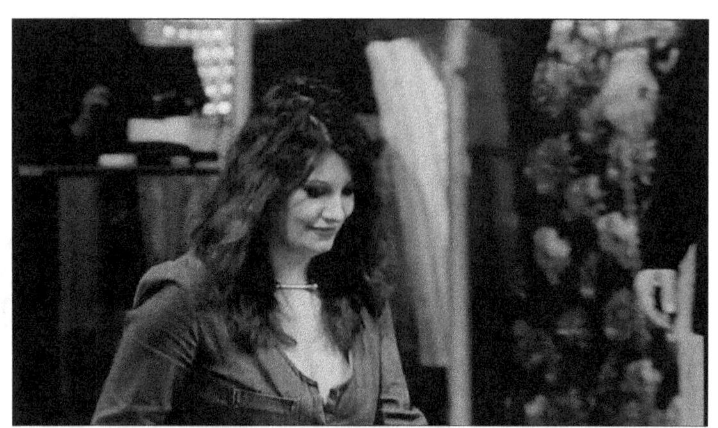

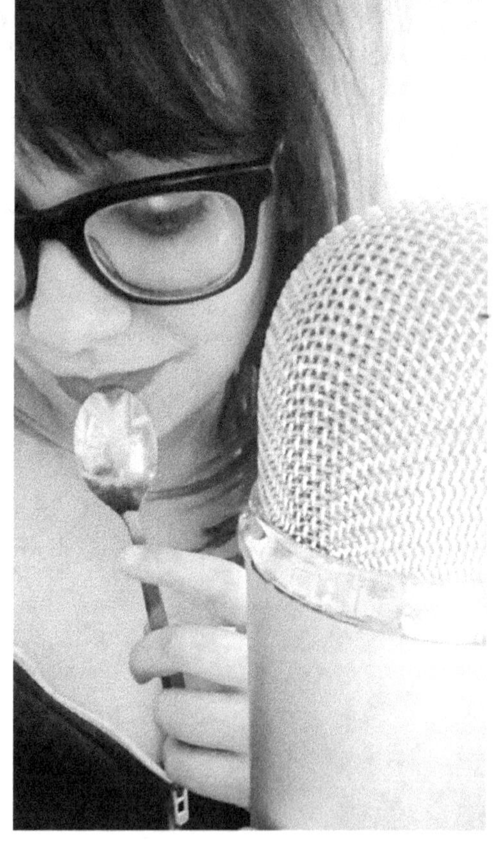

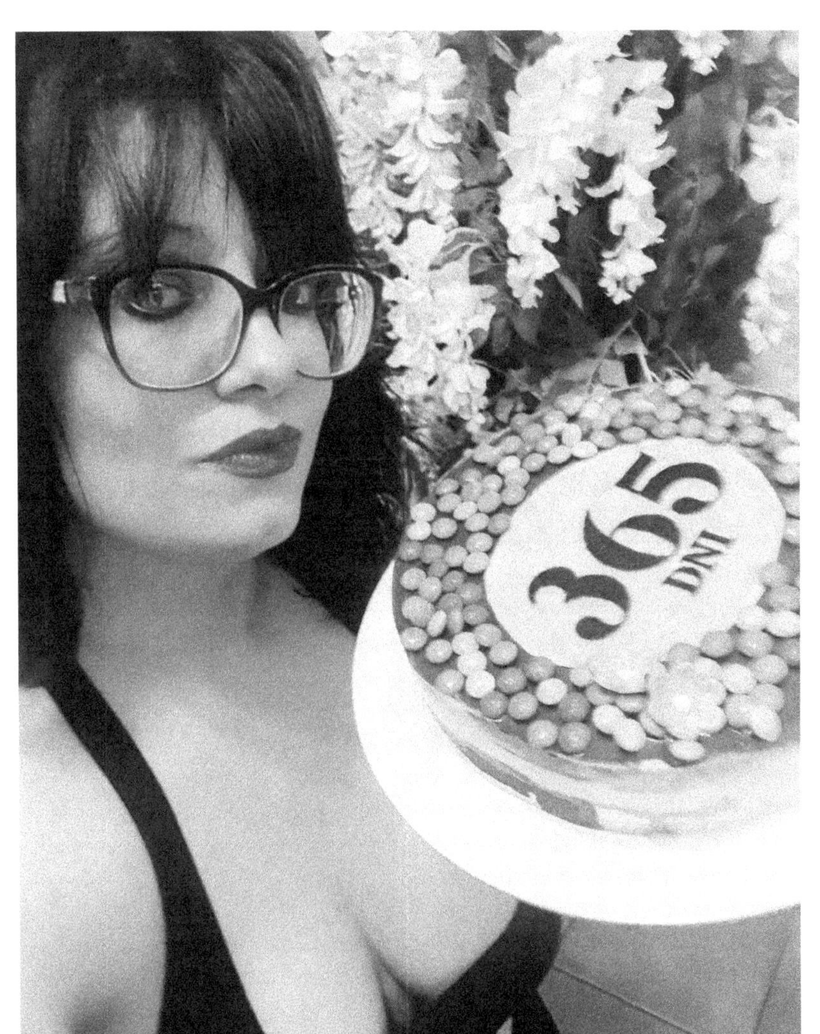

365
DNI

I WAIT FOR YOU IN MY YOUTUBE CHANNEL!

GIULIA   SEGRETI